DIAN FOSSEY

At Home With the Giant Gorillas

Corinne J. Naden and Rose Blue

A Gateway Green Biography
The Millbrook Press
Brookfield, Connecticut

To my favorite small people, Jason and Sara Schwarz,
love, "Mz" Corinne.

To my very talented young friend Ben Ratner,
love, Rose.

Cover photograph courtesy of © Dian Fossey Gorilla Fund International/P. Veit
Photographs courtesy of © Y. Arthus-Bertrand/Peter Arnold, Inc.: pp. 6, 14, 32, 35; © Robert I.
Campbell/NGS Image Collection: pp. 8, 19, 20, 21, 25, 27, 37; © Des Bartlett/NGS Image
Collection: p. 11; Photo Researchers, Inc.: pp. 12 (© George Holton), 23 (middle © Art Wolfe,
bottom © Eric & David Hosking); © Arthur Schatz/TimePix: p. 16; © Kennan Ward/Corbis: p. 17;
Peter Arnold, Inc.: pp. 23 (top © Tom Vezo), 39 (© Evelyn Gallardo), 41 (©BIOS/M. Gunther); ©
Peter Weit/Corbis Sygma: p. 29; © Dian Fossey/NGS Image Collection: p. 30; Photofest: p. 33

Library of Congress Cataloging-in-Publication Data
Naden, Corinne J.
Dian Fossey : at home with the giant gorillas / Corinne J. Naden and Rose Blue.
p. cm. — (Gateway green)
Includes bibliographical references (p.).
Summary: Profiles the life of the scientist who studied mountain gorillas in central Africa and
worked to ensure their survival.
ISBN 0-7613-2569-7 (lib. bdg.)
1. Fossey, Dian—Juvenile literature. 2. Primatologists—Biography—Juvenile literature. 3.
Gorilla—Juvenile literature. [1. Fossey, Dian. 2. Zoologists. 3. Gorilla. 4. Women—Biography.]
I. Blue, Rose. II. Title. III. Gateway green biography.
QL31.F65 N34 2002
599.884′092—dc21 [B] 2001044426

Published by The Millbrook Press
2 Old New Milford Road
Brookfield, Connecticut 06804
www.millbrookpress.com

DIAN FOSSEY

Dian Fossey

THE PLACE OF THE HANDS

It began just as any other day in the African jungle. She sat quietly on a tree trunk, almost hidden by the thick plant growth. She knew he was watching her. After a while, he left his group and wandered over. She said later he was wearing his "I want to be entertained" expression. Ever so slowly, she left her hiding spot. She picked up a plant and pretended to eat it. That was to tell him she meant no harm.

For a while he just watched with his bright staring eyes. Suddenly he sat down next to her. He seemed bored. She scratched her head. He scratched his. She could not be sure but maybe something was happening here.

Slowly she put out her hand, palm up. She rested it on the leaves and kept very still. He stared for a while. Then an amazing thing happened. He held out his own huge hand and touched her fingers. It was just for a moment, and then he ran off beating his chest with his hands.

*Dian interacts with Peanuts, the first
gorilla that touched her in 1970.*

She was Dian Fossey, American scientist, adventurer, and dreamer who became an expert on the endangered mountain gorilla. He was a young male gorilla whom she called Peanuts—a strong, hairy, gentle giant ape of the forest. The year was 1970. This spot where the first known friendly touch occurred between human and gorilla is called The Place of the Hands.

It took many hours and years of research and caring to connect Fossey and mountain gorillas. This is their story.

A LONELY START

"I had this great urge, this need to go to Africa," Dian Fossey said in an interview in 1983. "I had it the day I was born."

She was born in San Francisco, California, on January 16, 1932. Her childhood was unhappy and lonely. Her parents divorced when she was three years old. Dian's mother, Kitty, said that Dian's father had died. Actually, he just disappeared. Father and daughter met thirty years later, but they never became close. George Fossey committed suicide in 1968.

When Dian was five, her mother remarried. Her stepfather was Richard Price and he pretty much ignored her. Dian and her mother were not very close either.

For one thing, by the time Dian was fourteen, she had grown into an attractive teenager with dark hair and hazel eyes, who was over 6 feet (183 centimeters) tall. She was taller than both her mother and her stepfather. Kitty, a beautiful and petite fashion model, seemed embarrassed by her daughter's height. That made Dian feel very awkward.

Fossey spent a lot of time with horses in high school. She wanted to study veterinary medicine. In 1950, she enrolled at the University of California at Davis. She did not do well in chemistry and physics, however, so she flunked out. In 1954, she earned a degree in occupational therapy at San Jose State.

Where could she make a living and still be around horses? She did not want to stay in California. Kentucky, a state known for its horses, seemed a good choice. She became director of the occupational therapy department at Kosair Crippled Children's Hospital in Louisville. This is the home of the Kentucky Derby, America's most famous horse race.

During her eleven years at Kosair, Fossey was proud of the work she did in helping disabled children. Most of them were victims of polio, a crippling disease at that time.

Fossey was always a loner. She lived in a farm cottage about 10 miles (16 kilometers) from the city and collected stray animals. But she did become friends with a secretary on the Kosair staff, Mary Henry.

In 1960, Henry went to Africa to visit family friends. When she returned with photos of the animal life in Rhodesia (now Zimbabwe), Fossey was hooked. She just had to see Africa. How could she do it?

First she asked her parents for a loan. They refused such a crazy idea. Finally, in 1963, with a three-year bank loan for

$8,000 and seven weeks' vacation, Fossey set off on an African safari. She flew to Nairobi, Kenya, and found a guide, John Alexander, an ex–park warden.

FIRST VISIT TO AFRICA

Fossey and Alexander first stopped at the Olduvai Gorge in Tanzania. There she met Louis and Mary Leakey. These famous anthropologists had been studying Africa for more than thirty years.

Louis Leakey told Fossey about Jane Goodall, who was then studying chimpanzees in Tanzania. Goodall would become world famous for her research.

Louis Leakey (middle) working at the Olduvai Gorge in Tanzania

The gorilla is the largest living primate. An adult male mountain gorilla may weigh around 340 pounds (154 kilograms). The female weighs about 185 pounds (84 kilograms). Usually, they walk with their back feet and front knuckles on the ground.

Fossey told Leakey that she was interested in seeing the mountain gorilla. Leakey spoke of the need for research with those endangered animals. Fossey later said that the idea of studying the mountain gorilla was born in her at that moment.

She and Alexander headed for the Virunga volcano country in the Congo (later renamed Zaire). Before they left, she badly sprained her ankle. But Fossey had come too far to stop. Her injury made her all the more determined.

They drove for four days and stopped overnight at Traveller's Rest. Then, with a bandaged and aching foot, along with porters and two more guides, she made a six-and-a-half-hour climb up Mount Mikeno. There in the sunlight of Kabara Meadow in the Congo was Fossey's dream.

Several giant adult mountain gorillas were staring at the strangers. Their large dark eyes peered from leathery faces surrounded by thick black hair. If the gorillas had wanted to attack them, there was nothing the travelers could do.

Then, Fossey heard one of their piercing, high-pitched screams. She nearly ran right back down the mountain, sore foot and all. But she did not run, and this changed her life. She later wrote, "I was struck by the physical magnificence of the huge jet-black bodies blended against . . . the thick forest foliage."

A DREAM COME TRUE

When Fossey went back to Louisville, things were not the same. She continued working with the children at Kosair and began paying back her bank loan. But her mind and heart stayed in Africa with the mountain gorillas. Then, a miracle happened.

Louis Leakey arrived in Louisville on a lecture tour in early 1966. Fossey was afraid he would not remember her. Instead, he even remembered her injured ankle. He also recalled some articles she had published on the gorillas after her return from Africa in 1963.

Mountain gorillas relaxing and playing in their natural habitat

Leakey wanted to start field studies on these great apes. They were on the endangered list. Would Fossey become the "gorilla girl"?

Of course, she said yes. In fact, she could not believe her luck! But, first, Leakey had to obtain funding. He also told her she should have her appendix removed. There is little medical help in the African jungle.

Fossey had her appendix removed. It was only later that she learned Leakey had just been testing her determination. As she later said, that was her introduction to his "unique sense of humor."

While waiting for funding, Fossey quit her job and returned to her family in California. Her mother thought that Dian had completely lost her mind with this new plan. She would never understand her daughter's need to live in Africa. Fossey just called it fate.

Finally, a long eight months later, Dian got the word. The Wilkie Foundation, which had sponsored Goodall's study of chimpanzees, would sponsor Fossey's study of the mountain gorillas. A short time later, the National Geographic Society also agreed to help with funding.

Fossey packed four cameras, countless rolls of film, and a three-year supply of clothes. She said good-bye to family in California and friends in Louisville.

The night before her flight from Washington, D.C., she stayed at the home of Jane Goodall's mother. By this time Fossey had come down with pneumonia. So, on December 19, 1966, she took some medicine and boarded the plane. Never again would she call America her home.

In certain ways, Dian Fossey was not the best choice for this study. She was not in great health. A heavy smoker, she constantly wheezed. And she knew very little about Africa, mountain gorillas, or living in the wilderness. She could not speak the language and she was not a trained scientist. But she was certainly determined.

Fossey spent Christmas with Jane Goodall and Jane's husband. Goodall showed her how to organize a camp and collect data. In Nairobi, Africa, she met up with her friends Joan and Alan Root. They were nature photographers whom she had met in 1963.

The Roots helped her buy supplies. She also purchased a Land Rover she named Lily. Alan Root agreed to go with her to

Fossey's friends Joan and Alan Root

*British-born Jane Goodall became world famous for
her long-term research with chimpanzees at
Gombe Stream National Park in Tanzania.*

the Kabara Meadow to set up camp. In January 1967, Fossey was ready for the adventure of her life.

SETTING UP CAMP

Fossey set up her first campsite at Kabara Meadow in the Parc National des Virungas in the Congo. It was there, several years earlier, that American scientist George Schaller led a field study on the apes. He was the first to help change the gorilla's reputation from frightful monster to gentle giant. Another American scientist, Carl Akeley, also studied the apes of the Virungas. He is buried in the meadow. In the 1920s, Akeley created a national park to protect the gorillas.

It took forty-two porters to hike Fossey's gear up the mountain and set up camp. They created bathrooms and a drainage system. Her home and office was a tent 7 by 9 feet (2 by 3 meters). Later she moved to a cabin.

Root had arranged for a cook and a helper to join Fossey. He also provided a tracker named Sanweckwe to come to the camp every two weeks. Sanweckwe had tracked gorillas with Akeley. He became Fossey's valuable aide and friend.

He taught her how to survive in the jungle. He also gave her two chickens, which she named Lucy and Desi. Now she could have eggs. She also had geese, birds, and a big brown boxer dog named Cindy as companions.

It was time to get to work. For the next several months, Fossey observed the gorillas and sent monthly reports to

Fossey taking photographs with Cindy, one of her close companions

Leakey. But just as she felt she was gaining acceptance with the great apes, the reality of life in Africa came crashing down. A rebellion broke out in the Congo.

One morning in July, Fossey found her camp surrounded by armed soldiers. They forced her down the mountain and held her for two weeks. They said it was for her safety, but Fossey wondered if she would ever be released.

She bribed the guards into driving her to pick up her Land Rover. She told them all her money was in the car. Once over

Fossey buys supplies in a town in Rwanda

the border in Uganda, Fossey escaped from her guards. She went to the Travellers' Rest, where she had stayed in 1963.

Fossey heard that if she returned to the Congo, she would be shot. Where could she go? With Leakey's help, within weeks she was once again studying the gorillas in the Virungas. This time she decided to set up camp in the tiny country of Rwanda, which shares a border with the Congo.

After several days of travel in the Land Rover, she found the perfect spot for her new camp. On a high windy meadow between two mountains, she established the Karisoke Research Centre on September 24, 1967.

GETTING TO KNOW THE GORILLAS

Fossey had gone to Africa to study what the gorillas ate, their nesting habits, and other behaviors. This is not easy. Although

Fossey's new camp in the Virunga Mountains in Rwanda

the gorillas eat and travel in close groups, they usually run from strangers.

The first thing Fossey had to do was to get the gorillas used to her. She sat for hours hidden in the thick bushes. Eventually, when they were used to seeing her, she began to act like them. She thought this would make them more comfortable about her being there.

Who Are These Gentle Giants?

The gorilla belongs to the order of primates. So do humans. Primates have several things in common, such as a large brain and newborns that need a long period of care.

Gorillas are the largest of the anthropoid, or manlike, apes. The adult male mountain gorilla is about 5 feet 7 inches (170 centimeters) tall. The adult female is several inches shorter. Except for the chimpanzee, gorillas are the closest living relative to humans. All wild gorillas live in Africa.

Gorillas are usually not aggressive. They do not charge unless attacked or threatened. Once they have scared away an intruder, they return to their peaceful habits. They speak among themselves with grunts, hoots, and the unforgettable earsplitting roar of the male.

There are three subspecies of gorillas. The western lowland gorilla is called the *Gorilla gorilla gorilla*. The eastern lowland gorilla is the *Gorilla gorilla graueri*. And the most famous is the mountain gorilla, or *Gorilla gorilla beringei*.

The shy western lowland gorilla has small jaws and teeth. It lives in the Congo Basin. There are perhaps 40,000 of them.

The eastern lowland gorilla is the largest of the three subspecies. It has short black fur. There are between 4,000 and 10,000 in the Congo.

The mountain gorilla is the hairiest of the three. Its black hair is long and silky and covers most of its body. They survive in just two places in the world—the forests of Uganda and the Virunga Mountain region. This includes parts of Rwanda, Congo (formerly Zaire), and Uganda.

With a growing human population all around it, the mountain gorilla has been threatened with extinction. Today, there are about 600 left in the wild. There are none in captivity, that is, in zoos.

A western lowland gorilla

A mountain gorilla

An eastern lowland gorilla

23

Since she had no rules to go by, Fossey made her own. Sometimes, she was wrong. For instance, she imitated the way a gorilla beats its chest by slapping her hands against her thighs. This got the gorillas' attention, and Fossey began to think she was clever. Then she realized that chest-beating is a signal for alarm or excitement. This was not a message she wanted to send.

She was more successful with pretending to eat their favorite foods or pick bugs out of her hair. She even copied their sounds. When a gorilla made a deep belching sound, so did Fossey.

What Do Gorillas Eat?

Gorillas eat plants. They do not eat meat. Mountain gorillas in the Kabara eat about thirty different kinds of plants, but they are fussy about which ones. In fact, gorillas spend most of the day eating. The adult male eats about 50 pounds (23 kilograms) of plants during the day.

Gorillas really seem to enjoy eating. They often grumble contentedly while chewing. Sometimes they smack their lips together after a particularly tasty bite.

This method may have been unscientific, but it worked. It took time, but that's what fieldwork is all about. Eventually the gorillas accepted her. Sometimes they came within a few feet of

*At her camp, Fossey studies and takes notes on her
collection of gorilla bones and skulls.*

her. Sometimes they moved even closer to look at a camera bag
or pick up her knapsack.

And then, some two years into her fieldwork, there was
Peanuts. When Peanuts touched her hand, Fossey later said,
that moment was one of the "most memorable of my life
among the gorillas."

Over the next few years, Karisoke truly became Fossey's home
and her life. She stopped writing to family and friends in the

United States. She did keep in contact with Leakey, who was worried about her safety. After all, she was one woman living alone in the wild. The local people called her *"Nyiramachabelli"*—the woman who lives alone on the mountain.

Leakey was also worried about her health. She now lived in a rain forest where sunshine reaches the ground only a few days during the winter. Some of her teeth fell out. Her feet grew moldy. Maybe, Leakey suggested, she should go down the mountain for a while.

In 1971, Fossey did go down the mountain, but not for health reasons. It had always bothered her that she did not have a degree to study animals. So she entered Cambridge University in England to earn a doctoral degree.

She hated being away from her gorillas and traveled back as often as she could. In the meantime, she set up a program to keep the Karisoke Research Centre running.

Finally, in 1976, she completed her studies. She was now Dr. Dian Fossey. She made a brief trip to California to visit her parents. She also attended a conference sponsored by the National Geographic Society. Then Dr. Dian Fossey returned to Karisoke and the apes.

Certainly there were times on her mountaintop when Fossey was lonely—even afraid. But for the most part, she found great joy in her life among the gorillas. She grew very close to them. Just as people have special friends, several of these animals

Dian became very close friends with the gorillas she lived among.

became special to her. She began to see that, just like people, gorillas had their own personalities.

There was Peanuts, of course. Along with two other young males, Geezer and Samson, Peanuts would often climb up a tree where Fossey sat with her camera. The three apes would check out her photographic equipment. Sometime after the first contact with Fossey in 1970, Peanuts wandered away from the study area. He wandered back in 1977, fifteen years old and a mature male.

Puck was often the first of his group to show he was bored. So Fossey tried to amuse him. He liked to look through her binoculars. Fossey once gave him a copy of *National Geographic* magazine. He flipped through the pages and especially enjoyed the color pictures.

DIGIT

Fossey first met another ape that became her special friend in September 1967, when he was about five years old. He was a small ball of black fluff with a bent middle finger. She named him Digit.

They formed a strong bond. One day Fossey found him separated from the rest of the group. She sat down a short distance away. Before long, she felt an arm around her shoulders. Then Digit patted her on the head and sat down next to her.

Digit was curious about everything. He examined all her equipment very carefully. He often spent time peering into her hand mirror and seemed pleased with his image. However, Fossey did not know if he actually recognized himself. Today, studies show that humans, apes, and dolphins are the only creatures able to see themselves as individuals in a mirror.

Fossey did think, however, that Digit recognized the difference between male and female visitors. He would charge at men in a playful way. With women, he acted shy.

The gorillas loved to inspect Fossey's equipment, but normally she didn't give them objects that were not native to the jungle.

Digit was one of Fossey's most beloved friends.

In 1971, Fossey made Digit famous without meaning to. The Rwanda tourist office asked her for a photograph of a gorilla that would attract visitors to the park. Fossey gave them a picture of Digit. It was made into posters and advertised all over the world, reading "Come and See Me in Rwanda!"

Fossey began to fear that the publicity would threaten the gorillas. She already had more visitors than she sometimes wanted. But what happened on December 31, 1977, was much worse. Courageous Digit was killed by poachers, people who hunt animals illegally. Before he died, Digit fought off the six poachers and their dogs, allowing his own family to escape.

Fossey buried Digit near her cabin, but her life was changed. She said that after Digit's death, she drew more into herself. Rumors spread that she had a nervous breakdown. She said she just could not allow herself to think about what happened to her beloved friend.

She and her student volunteers, who had come to study with her, decided to count the mountain gorilla population. They found only 242 gorillas. This was a big drop in number from the last count more than twenty years earlier. Fossey was convinced that poachers and trophy hunters were mostly responsible.

Poachers roam the jungle setting traps and snares. Fossey began to spend her time removing the traps. She burned the poachers' camps and threw away their food. Fossey was becoming a threat. She set up a Digit Fund to raise money to fight the poachers.

Dian poses near her cabin with armed guards
who protect her and help confiscate poachers' slings,
or traps, which are piled in front of them.

By 1979, Fossey had new worries. The government of
Rwanda was threatening to turn Karisoke into a tourist attrac-
tion. The Leakey Foundation—Louis Leakey himself had died
in 1972—wanted her to return to the United States to write

about her research. If she did not, they threatened to cut off funding.

So Fossey accepted a teaching position at Cornell University in New York. She stayed there for three years. Her students found her distant, perhaps because her heart remained in Africa.

During this time she wrote *Gorillas in the Mist*. This was about her thirteen years in the rain forest with the great apes. In 1988, it was made into a movie.

Sigourney Weaver played Dian Fossey in the movie version of Gorillas in the Mist. *Weaver received an Academy Award nomination for her role.*

What Have We Learned?

Dian Fossey focused on about fifty-one apes living in four families not far from her camp. What have we learned from her work?

Each gorilla family group is led by a dominant male silverback, so called because of the silver hair that grows across his back as he ages. A group travels together and usually contains from five to twenty members.

A typical small family group may have a silverback, three adult females, a young male, and two or three youngsters. A large group may have about forty members with three or more silverbacks. However, one silverback in the group is dominant and is rarely challenged by another gorilla. His size alone is usually threat enough.

The silverback takes care of the group. He defends them from hunters or perhaps a large leopard that threatens the family. He is also generally tolerant of infant gorillas when they crawl all over him.

The male gorilla usually will begin to breed when he is between fifteen and twenty years old. The female gorilla gives birth for the first time at about ten years old. Like humans, she usually has only one baby at a time.

Gorilla babies weigh only about 4 pounds (2 kilograms) when they are born. Like human babies, they are totally dependent upon the mother. For the first few months, they travel the forest by clinging to the hair on the mother's chest.

Gorillas live to be thirty years or more in the jungle. They may die of disease or accidents or a fight with a ferocious leopard. But humans are their worst enemies.

Poachers, trophy hunters, and those who value gorilla parts are the enemy. But so is the ever-expanding human population that threatens the gorillas' grazing range. If mountain gorillas can no longer roam the rain forests for their food, they will all die.

MORE TRAGEDY STRIKES

By 1983, Fossey was back at Karisoke. But she was a changed woman. She almost totally isolated herself from other humans. She preferred the company of the apes. Preserving them became her goal and her obsession.

"Dian was a very strong lady," said Ruth Reesling, who met Fossey in 1984 at a conference sponsored by the San Diego Zoo. "The move to keep animals in captivity interested Dian," Reesling said. "She felt it was necessary to change exhibits in zoos to suit the needs of gorillas. At the time she told me there were 248 mountain gorillas left in the world. She said they were all going to die and she was going to die with them if something was not done about poachers. She had a great relationship with the gorillas."

Although Fossey was back with her gorillas, she was not in good health. She limped from a broken leg that had healed poorly. Her lungs were so bad that she could no longer trek through the jungle for hours. She breathed with the help of an oxygen tank. Even so, she continued to smoke heavily.

Just past fifty years of age, she seemed old and frail. Yet she was no less determined to protect the gorillas of Karisoke. From time to time student volunteers continued to assist her.

When graduate student Wayne McGuire arrived in August 1985, she acknowledged that he had probably heard frightening stories about her. The best thing to do, she said, was to "ignore them and concentrate on the gorillas."

Fossey took care of two young gorillas after they were captured and seriously injured by poachers, who intended to sell them to a zoo. At the time, Pucker was a two-year-old female and Coco was a sixteen-month-old male.

Gorillas are social, gentle, and intelligent animals. Perhaps those traits caused Fossey to say, when she returned to Africa for the last time, "I know now that I've truly come home. No one will ever force me out of here again."

Fossey herself did not stop concentrating on the apes until the morning of December 27, 1985. McGuire heard one of the staff shouting in Swahili, *"Dian kufa kufa,"* or *"Dian is dead."*

When McGuire reached Dian's cabin, he found a ghastly sight. She had been killed with a large jungle knife called a panga. Nothing had been stolen. The purpose of the murder was not robbery.

Nine months later, authorities charged McGuire and five Rwandans with the crime. They claimed the motive was to obtain the research Fossey had gathered.

McGuire left Rwanda before the trial began. But the trial continued without him there, and he was convicted and sentenced to death. McGuire still denies the charges, saying there was no possible motive for him to have killed Fossey.

If McGuire didn't kill her, then who did? Most people think it was poachers, who hated Fossey. They use panga knives in their work. Others point out that Fossey had enemies in Africa. People who use gorillas for moneymaking purposes wanted her out of the way, too.

Wayne McGuire in Rwanda before he was convicted
of murdering Fossey. There are still many different
theories about who actually killed her.

Fossey no longer guards the gorillas of the mountain. But research on the apes continues. The Digit Fund is now the Dian Fossey Gorilla Fund. It works with countries all over the world to save the animals from extinction.

The Parc National des Volcans is a national park and is protected by Rwandan laws. Tourism has increased, and small groups are allowed to watch and to photograph the gorillas.

The local people, thanks perhaps to Fossey's work, appreciate these animals more. This put pressure on the poachers to leave them alone. But poachers and trophy hunters still roam the forests.

Another serious threat comes from the country itself. During the 1990s, Rwanda was torn by internal war, mainly between Tutsi and Hutu tribes. Work at the Karisoke Research Centre was shut down for most of 1998 because the staff could not enter the area.

In 2000, an uneasy peace came to Rwanda with the election of its first Tutsi president. But conservationists still worry about the fate of the apes. "No mountain gorillas will survive if Rwandans and non-Rwandans don't work together," a former director of Karisoke said.

Despite the obstacles, people and organizations are dedicated to protecting the mountain gorilla. According to Ruth Reesling, there are now about 620 of them in the park reserve.

Dian Fossey is buried next to her family—not the Fossey family, but the family of the great apes she loved. She rests forever in the Africa of her dreams, near her beloved Digit. Fossey loved the natural splendor and solitude of Rwanda. "Anywhere you look," she once said, "there is beauty."

Dian Fossey's grave in Rwanda

Chronology

1932   Fossey is born on January 16.

1950   She enrolls at the University of California at Davis to study veterinary medicine.

1952   She flunks out and enrolls at San Jose State.

1954   She graduates from San Jose State and works in Louisville.

1963   She makes her first trip to Africa, meets Louis Leakey, and sees mountain gorillas for the first time.

1966   Leakey asks Fossey to do research on mountain gorillas in Africa; she arrives in Africa in December.

1967   Internal war forces Fossey from the Congo; she establishes the Karisoke Research Centre in Rwanda.

1970   She makes contact with Peanuts.

1971   She enters Cambridge to study for a doctorate.

1976   She earns her doctoral degree and returns to Africa.

1977   Digit is murdered.

1980   She begins three years of teaching at Cornell University and begins writing *Gorillas in the Mist*.

1983   She returns to Karisoke.

1985   Fossey is murdered on December 27.

To Find Out More

Associations

American Zoo and Aquarium Association
8403 Colesville Rd., Suite 710
Silver Spring, MD 20910-3314
www.aza.org

The Dian Fossey Gorilla Fund International
800 Cherokee Ave., SE
Atlanta, Georgia 30315-1440
www.gorillafund.org

Books

Jerome, Leah. *Dian Fossey*. New York: Skylark, 1991.

Lewin, Ted. *Gorilla Walk*. New York: Lothrop Lee & Shepard, 1999.

Matthews, Tom. *Light Shining Through the Mist*. Washington, DC: National Geographic, 1998.

Miller-Schroder, Pat. *Gorillas*. Austin, TX: Raintree/Steck-Vaughn, 1997.

Patterson, Francine. *Koko-Love!: Conversations with a Signing Gorilla*. New York: Dutton Books, 1999.

Schott, Jane A. *Dian Fossey and the Mountain Gorillas*. New York: Carolrhoda, 2000.

Simon, Seymour. *Gorillas*. New York: Harpercollins, 2000.

Web sites

Dian Fossey and the Gorillas of the Virungas Volcanoes
www.unmuseum.org/fossey.htm

Dian Fossey Gorilla Fund
www.gorillas.org

Earthkeeper Heroes
http://www.myhero.com/earthkeepers/earthkeepers_content.asp

The Gorilla Foundation
www.gorilla.org

Primates Online
http://www.primates-online.com/

Works Consulted

Ake, Anne. *The Gorilla*. San Diego: Lucent, 1999.

"Dian Fossey." *Current Biography Yearbook*, 1985.

Fossey, Dian. *Gorillas in the Mist*. Boston: Houghton Mifflin, 1983.

Gorillas. San Diego: Zoobooks, 2000.

"Gorillas." *Encyclopedia Britannica*, Vol. 5. Chicago: University of Chicago Press, 1992.

"King of the Apes." *Encyclopedia of Mammals*, Vol. 6. London: Cavendish, 1997.

Lindsay, Jennifer. *The Great Apes*. New York: Metro, 1999.

Index

About the Authors

Corinne J. Naden is a former children's book editor and U.S. Navy journalist. She has published more than seventy-five books. Now a freelance writer, she lives in Tarrytown, New York, with her two cats, Tigger and Tally.

Rose Blue, an author and educator, has written more than eighty books, both fiction and nonfiction, for young readers. Her books have appeared as TV specials and have won many awards. A native New Yorker, she lives in the borough of Brooklyn.

The authors have written many books together, including *Christa McAuliffe: Teacher in Space, Benjamin Banneker: Mathematician and Stargazer, Colin Powell: Straight to the Top*, and *Jonas Salk: Polio Pioneer*, which are all part of the Gateway Biography series.